LIVERPOOL FROM THE AIR

LIVERPOOL FROM THE AIR

WEBBAVIATION.CO.UK

breedon **books** PUBLISHING

First published in Great Britain in 2007 by
The Breedon Books Publishing Company Limited
Breedon House, 3 The Parker Centre,
Derby, DE21 4SZ.

ISBN 978-1-85983-589-0

Printed and bound in Slovenia

Acknowledgments

There are a number of people who have helped in the making of this book and I would like to express particular thanks to the following: the UK's best photo pilot John Seville, who always manages to have the aircraft in exactly the right attitude and location at every site. The always helpful National Air Traffic Control Service at Liverpool's John Lennon airport, who manage to juggle airliners, training aircraft and aerial photographers all in the same bit of sky. Fellow aerial photographers Catherine Wheildon and William Cross for their constant support and friendship.

Contents

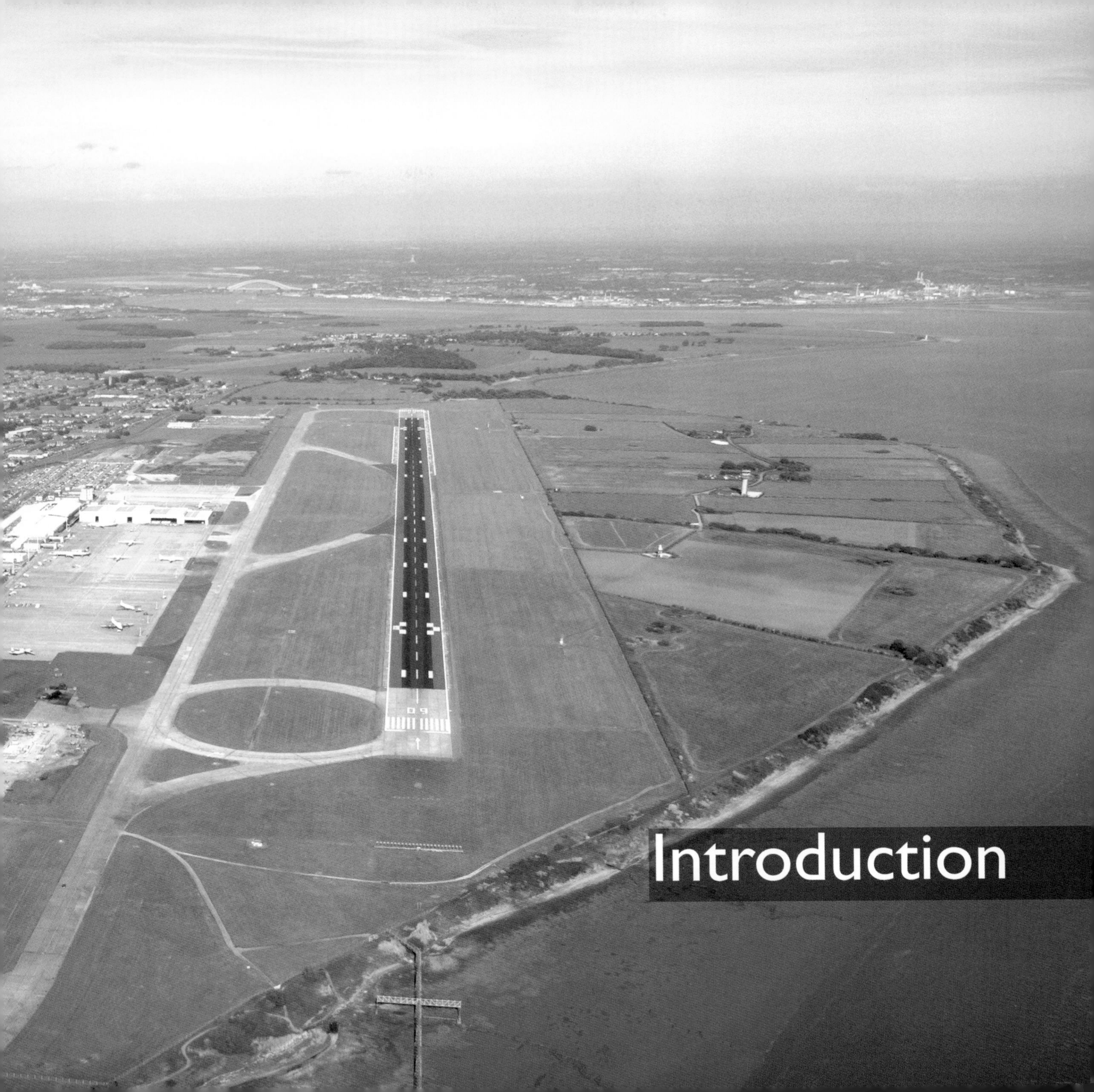

Introduction

Founded in 1207, Liverpool has a long and interesting past. In the 19th century the city became the 'second Port of the Empire' and one of the world's busiest ports. The mid-20th century saw a period of decline, but by the end of the century the city was back on the up and my images capture something of its rebirth, while still paying homage to the city's historical past.

Liverpool is incorporated within the Metropolitan County of Merseyside from which I have selected a variety of subjects, from the beauty and tranquility of Hilbre Island to the historically important docks at Birkenhead.

Culture

Liverpool Anglican Cathedral

The Cathedral Church of Christ in Liverpool was designed by Giles Gilbert Scott, who was only 22 at the time. Construction of the cathedral began in 1904 with a foundation stone laid by King Edward VII. The design was changed part way through construction from an original twin-towered design to the single tower we see today. The cathedral was completed in 1978 and is now the second biggest Anglican cathedral in the world, containing the world's highest and heaviest ringing peal of bells and, with 9,765 pipes, the largest working church organ in the world.

Liverpool Catholic Cathedral

Properly called the Liverpool Metropolitan Cathedral of Christ the King, the building was started in 1933 to a massive classical design by Sir Edwin Lutyens. This was the second attempt following a previous failed design by Edward Welby Pugin, but again work was halted after construction had started, this time due to the war and post-war financial problems. Only the crypt had been completed and so the cathedral was then redesigned in a modern style by Sir Fredrick Gibberd incorporating Lutyens's crypt which was built in just five years from 1962 to 1967, although steps were only added recently.

Former Liverpool Royal Infirmary

Originally the Liverpool Royal Infirmary, the buildings are now used by the University of Liverpool. It was designed in the Gothic Revival style by Liverpool-born architect Sir Alfred Waterhouse. The original building was much extended and used until 1978, when the hospital was relocated to a new hospital building nearby. Since the acquisition by the university the main buildings have undergone an extensive restoration and are now Grade II listed.

Chinese Arch

The Chinese Arch is the largest outside China. It was built in China to celebrate the year 2000 and shipped from Liverpool's twin city Shanghai to be assembled on-site by a team of Chinese craftsmen. The city has had a large Chinese community since the 19th century, making it the oldest in Europe. The arch is 15 metres high with 200 dragons and five roofs.

Merseyside Maritime Museum

The former Liverpool pilot cutter the *Edmund Gardner* is the largest exhibit of the Liverpool Maritime Museum. From 1953 to 1982 she enabled pilots to guide incoming shipping into the Mersey Docks. The two dry docks in which she sits are the oldest surviving graving docks in Liverpool and were built in 1765–68 as part of the Canning Dock. In graving dock no. 2 is the last commercial sailing ship to trade to the Mersey, the three-masted schooner *De Wadden*, built in 1917. Above the graving docks is the Great Western Railway building and at the bottom of the shot is the propeller from the Cunard liner *Lusitania*.

Historic Warships Museum

Now sadly closed, the Historic Warships Museum stood on the other side of the Mersey at Birkenhead until 2006. In the photograph is the submarine HMS *Onyx*, which carried SAS troops in the Falklands War, and HMS *Plymouth* onboard which the surrender of South Georgia took place. To the right is U-boat U-534, which was raised from the seabed.

Sefton Park

Opened in 1872 on land bought from the Earl of Sefton, the park was designed in a French style by Edouard Andre and local architect Lewis Hornblower. The Grade II listed Palm House, which opened in 1896, is of particular interest and contains plant species from all over the world. The Palm House underwent a multi-million pound restoration between 2000 and 2001 and is now used for a variety of concerts and events, including a monthly tea dance.

Liverpool Arena

Opening in 2008, the Liverpool Arena and convention centre will provide a new venue for events, with a capacity for over 10,000. The arena also includes a 1,350-seat conference centre and 7,600sq m exhibition hall. It is built on the former Kings Dock, which closed in 1972 and is now subject to this massive redevelopment that will include hotel, retail and residential areas.

St Lukes Church, Berry Street

Berry Street was originally laid out as a rope walk – a long narrow piece of land used in the manufacture of rope for the rigging of sailing ships of the day. The area was bombed on the night of 5 May 1941 and St Luke's Church was burnt out. The church now stands as a memorial to those who lost their lives in the blitz. It was built from 1811 to 1831 to a design by John Foster.

The Big Top

The Big Top Arena at Clarence Dock is used as a temporary venue for Liverpool's annual Summer Pops festival. Established in 2001 with 30 shows every July, the hugely popular Summer Pops are attended by over 100,000 visitors. The 4,500-seat arena has hosted a wide variety of performers from Brian Wilson to Bryan Adams. In 2008 the festival will move to the new Liverpool Arena.

Liverpool John Moores University

Founded in 1825 as the Liverpool Mechanics' School of Arts, the university grew to become Liverpool Polytechnic which was renamed Liverpool John Moores University in 1992. The buildings of the university are dispersed over a wide area of Liverpool and the Wirral. One of the key areas is the Mount Pleasant Campus in this image. University buildings here include the Joe H. Makin Drama Centre, the distinctive new Aldham Robarts Learning Centre, the Haigh Building, the Hahnemann Building, Blackburne Place and Josephine Butler House.

The University of Liverpool

Established in 1881 as the University College Liverpool, it became the University of Liverpool in 1903. The university has over 23,000 registered students and has produced eight Nobel Prize winners.

Left: the new £25 million Biosciences Centre opened in 2003, providing facilities for research and new biotech businesses.

Overleaf: the university precinct almost surrounds the Metropolitan Cathedral.

Docks and Shipping

Shipping

Liverpool was founded on shipping by King John in 1207 and takes its name from a tidal pool, which was used for shipping and lay underneath the building site in the centre of the image on the previous page . Often referred to as 'The second port of the empire', the port reached its peak in the late 19th century when it controlled a seventh of the world's shipping and was second only to London in the UK. Both Cunard and White Star Line were based in the port and famous ships included the *Titanic* and the *Lusitania*.

Previous page: Liverpool South Docks, city centre and Birkenhead across the Mersey.

Left: A buoy moored in the River Mersey.

Right: The radar-equipped coastal watch oversees shipping entering the Mersey.

Shipping

Even today Liverpool is a very important port, handling most of the UK's container trade with North America and bulk cargoes such as grain and oil. Trade reached a new record of 32,226,000 tonnes in 2004.

Above: Bulk Carrier *Clara* unloading at the Royal Seaforth Dock.

Left clockwise from top: Oil tanker *Navion Oceania*, tugboat *Svitzer Stanlow* and the French general cargo vessel *Delphine Delmas*.

Albert Docks

Opened in 1846 by Prince Albert, whose name the dock carries, it is now Britain's largest group of Grade I listed buildings. Designed by Jesse Hartley to be non-combustible, they were built entirely of cast iron, stone and brick. The docks finally closed in 1972 but in the early 1980s were restored and they now contain the Maritime Museum, the Tate Liverpool art gallery and 'The Beatles Story' exhibition.

Previous page: Container unloading at Royal Seaforth Dock.
Opposite: The Albert Docks.
Above: Now used for ship repairs, the former Cammell-Laird shipyards in Birkenhead had built some of the world's greatest ships, including the world's first steel ship and the liner *Mauritania*.

Birkenhead Docks

By the 19th century as Liverpool grew there came a need for expansion and Birkenhead on the other side of the Mersey had a number of advantages, including deeper water and shelter from the wind by hills. The first docks to open were the Morpeth and Egerton docks in 1847, with numerous other docks added in the following years in response to growing trade, particularly in livestock and grain. It was from here that emigrants set sail for new lives in the colonies. In recent years trade has declined and there are plans to redevelop the whole area with numerous skyscrapers in the 'Wirral Waters' scheme.

Huskisson Dock

Opened in 1852 for the timber trade, the Huskinsson dock is still in use today. In the late 19th and early 20th century the dock was used for Cunard liners on the North American run. In 1909 the Cunard luxury liner *Lucania* was destroyed by fire here and in 1941 during the Blitz a steamer, the SS *Malakand*, loaded with 1,000 tons of explosive, caught fire and exploded, destroying the dock and with some parts of the ship ending up 2½ miles away. In the 1950s the dock was used for sugar and the huge silo, top left of the image, was built. Today the dock handles oil and general cargo.

Waterloo Dock

Built in 1834 by French prisoners of war, the dock was originally designed as a general cargo dock for sailing ships. The grain warehouses, the world's first to be mechanically operated, were added in 1868 at a cost of £559,000. There were originally three warehouse blocks, but the north block was destroyed in the Blitz of May 1941 and the west block was demolished in 1969 to make way for a new container terminal. The docks closed in 1988 and have since been redeveloped, with the Grade II listed Waterloo Warehouse being converted into 218 luxury apartments which won the 1991 RIBA Design Award.

Previous: The Royal Seaforth Docks.

Royal Seaforth Docks

Opened in 1972, the Royal Seaforth was the last of Liverpool's docks to be completed. The docks were built for the larger vessels of up to 70,000 tons in 10 berths for grain, timber and containers. In 1984 business was further boosted when the docks became a Freeport, where goods can be stored without paying taxes. The wind farm was added in 1999 and its six turbines generate 3.6 mega watts of electricity, or enough for around 2,000 houses. There are also plans to significantly extend this capacity.

Clarence Graving Docks

Designed by Jesse Hartley and opened in 1830, the Grade II listed structures are the oldest docks still in service on the Mersey. In 1865 the *Mimosa* was prepared here to take Welsh emigrants to a new life in Patagonia, where their descendents still live. The steamship in the bottom left of the image is the preserved tug tender *Daniel Adamson* undergoing restoration.

Above: Centre Collingwood Dock, to its left the Salisbury Dock and above it Nelson Dock.

Princes Half Tide Dock

Even in the 21st century, the future of all of Liverpool's historic docks is uncertain. Here we see Princes Half Tide dock, opened in 1821, being filled with rubble, although it may be reopened later with a proposed canal link between the north and south docks.

Princes Dock

The landing stage here in the 19th century was the world's longest floating structure. The dock was used for loading and unloading cargo from many of the great liners before they embarked passengers from the landing stage, many of them emigrating to the US.

The Tobacco Warehouse

Stanley Dock, opened in 1848, was originally square in shape. It was partially filled in 1901 to allow the construction of the massive, Grade II listed Tobacco Warehouse. At the time it was claimed to be the world's largest building, with 14 stories and 27 million bricks used in its construction. It became disused in the 1980s and now faces an uncertain future.

Isle of Man - Steam Packet

Started in 1830, the Isle of Man Steam Packet Company is the oldest continuously operating, passenger shipping company in the world. The company's new high-speed ferry, the *Superseacat II*, seen here, does the crossing from Liverpool to the Isle of Man in only two and a half hours.

Overleaf: The Mersey Ferry *Royal Daffodil*. Made famous in the 1964 song *Ferry across the Mersey* by Gerry and The Pacemakers, the Mersey Ferries still make a scheduled crossing of the river despite the construction of the three tunnels. There are also regular cruises up the river and the Manchester Ship Canal.

Sport

Royal Liverpool Golf Course - Hoylake

Opened in 1869 on the site of the Liverpool Hunt Club Racecourse, which ran concurrently for a number of years. The course received its 'Royal' title from Queen Victoria's son, the Duke of Connaught, in 1871. In 2006 the course played host to the Open Championships, which were won by Tiger Woods.

Aintree

Home of the Grand National, the first race was held here in 1829 and the first Grand National in 1839. The horse-racing course is accompanied by a motor-racing circuit, which opened in 1953 and has since hosted five Grand Prix one of which was the first win by Stirling Moss. Within the race-courses lies the Aintree golf centre, which has a nine-hole course and a driving range.

Previous page: Sea fog drifts in over northern Liverpool towards the Everton stadium.

Anfield - Liverool Football Club

Originally the home of Everton Football Club, who vacated the stadium when the rent was increased, Liverpool Football club was set up in 1892 by club chairman John Houlding using the now-vacant stadium. The club has gone on to be one of Britain's most successful, becoming League Champions 18 times, League Cup winners seven times, FA Cup winners seven times, European Cup winners five times and UEFA Cup winners three times. The club is now likely to leave Anfield for a new stadium to be built nearby.

Goodison Park - Everton Football Club

Started in 1878 and originally named St Domingo FC after the local church and school, the club was renamed Everton in 1879. Goodison Park was the country's first purpose-built football stadium and was completed in 1892. The club is one of the top clubs in England and have won the Football League First Division nine times, the FA Cup five times as well as being European Cup winners in 1984–85. The club is now looking at the possibility of having a new stadium built in a different part of Liverpool.

Architecture

The Three Graces

Previous page: Three of Liverpool's most important buildings sit side by side at Pier Head and are known collectively as the Three Graces. They are, from left to right above: The Royal Liver Building, the Cunard Building and the Port of Liverpool Building.

Above, left and overleaf: The Royal Liver Building, by Walter Aubrey Thomas. Britain's first skyscraper, its 13 floors were constructed in 1908-11 using the then-revolutionary technique of reinforced concrete. The buildings are crowned with two mythical Liver Birds, which were designed by German artist Carl Bernard Bartels.

Liver Birds

Cunard Building

The second of the Three Graces is the Cunard Building, pictured here in the middle, which was constructed between 1914 and 1916 to a Italianate design by Willinck and Thicknesse, with Arthur J. Davis as consultant. The Grade II listed building remained home to Cunard until they moved to Southampton in the 1960s. Curiously, as you can see in the photograph, it is wider at the back than at the front.

Port of Liverpool Building

The Mersey Docks and Harbour Board offices, now known as the Port of Liverpool Building, were built in 1903-07. They were designed by Briggs and Wolstenholme, F.B. Hobbs and A. Thornely, who won a design competition for the building.

Beetham Tower West

This 40-storey 147 metre tower by Aedas architects and constructed by Carillion is Liverpool's tallest building and is seen here nearing completion in early 2007.

The Princes Dock area

The Princes Dock area is now undergoing major reconstruction, with numerous high-rise buildings being built.

Above: Alexandra Tower early in its construction in 2006.
Right: No. One Princes Dock both by AFL Architects.

Footbridge

The footbridge crossing Princes Dock was built in 2001 to a competition-wining design by Eduard Ross and Ian Wroot.

Castle Street

The commercial heart of the city, Castle Street is known for its wonderful architecture which currently provides a home to numerous banks. Note the narrow back alleys running at right angles to Castle Street and providing access to many smaller workshops and warehouses. Central in the image is the Grade II listed Nat West Bank, built to a design by Richard Norman Shaw with Willink and Thinknesse. On the corner with its back to camera is the Grade I listed Bank of England by C.R. Cockerell. With the green onion dome is W.D. Caroe's Grade II Adelphi Bank of 1892.

India Buildings

The Grade II listed India Buildings on Water Street were constructed between 1924 and 1931 for the Blue Funnel Line at a cost of £1,250,000 and to a design by Herbert J. Rowse, who was responsible for a number of Liverpool's greatest buildings. The hollow design which was common in buildings of the period allows natural daylight to penetrate to most internal areas.

The Collegiate

The Collegiate is a bold scheme by Shed KM and Urban Splash to rescue the fire damaged, grade II listed former school and find a new use as apartments.

Municipal Buildings

Built 1862–66 the Grade II listed buildings were designed by Corporation Surveyors John Weightman and E.R. Robson to accommodate the increasing numbers of local authority workers. The buildings were originally larger, with the back elevation having now been lost.

Liverpool Royal Infirmary

Left and previous page: Dominating the north-eastern corner of Liverpool city centre is the Royal Liverpool University Hospital, which was built to replace the Victorian buildings of the Liverpool Royal Infirmary. Constructed between 1966 and 1978, it reflects the functional architectural style of the period which contrasts starkly with the original Alfred Waterhouse design.

Martins Bank

Completed in 1932, this was another design by Herbert Rowse and is still fulfilling its original purpose to this day as a branch of Barclays Bank, who took over Martins Bank Ltd in 1969.

The Wellington Column and The Steble Fountain

Wellington's Column was designed by George Anderson Lawton of Glasgow and depicts Wellington atop a fluted Doric column with battle reliefs of his famous victories at Talevera, Vitoria, Badajoz and Waterloo. The fountain was a gift from Colonel R.F. Steble, who was the Mayor of Liverpool from 1874 to 1875.

Paradise Street

This is one of the UK's largest city centre redevelopment programs, with 42 acres being regenerated. The project includes 40 new, individually designed buildings and over 1.6 million square feet of retail space. On a historical note, the bottom left of the photograph opposite is the site of Old Dock, the world's first enclosed wet dock which was opened in 1715 and built in the Pool from which Liverpool gets its name. The dock was filled in during the middle of the 19th century but still lies there buried to this day.

William Brown Street

The street is unusual in that it only contains libraries, museums and galleries. They are, from left to right: The World Museum Liverpool (1860), Picton Reading Room and Hornby Library (1875–1906), the Walker Art Gallery (1877) and the former County Sessions Court (1884).

The Met Quarter

Built as the old Post Office in 1899, it was designed by Henry Tanner to resemble a Loire chateau. Following the closure of the Post Office, the outer lower walls have been incorporated in the new £75 million Met Quarter Shopping centre.

Radio City Tower

Formerly known as St Johns Beacon, the 133 metre high tower was built in 1965 as a ventilation tower for the market underneath. Designed by Weightman & Bullen Architects, it originally featured a revolving restaurant and is now used as a base for a local radio station.

Victoria Monument

The Victoria Monument by C.J. Allen was built in 1906, on the site of Liverpool Castle. The castle was constructed in the 13th century and much fought over during the English Civil War (1642-51), changing hands several times. At the end of the war the castle was 'slighted' and then demolished altogether in 1725. During construction of the Law Courts (left), a defensive ditch was uncovered which is thought to date from these battles.

Speke Hall

Most of the hall we see today dates from the period between 1490 and 1612, but there is also evidence of an earlier property at the site. The house was extensively restored in the mid 19th century and was passed to the National Trust in 1943. The hall is open to the public and is a popular venue for weddings.

Circle 109

Right: Part of the regeneration of the Rope Walks area of Liverpool, this apartment complex by Pierce Homes is constructed on a steel frame, clad in stone render, copper and glazing sections to a design by Falconer Chester Hall Architects.

Victoria Tower

Time is very important for navigation and the Victoria Tower was built as a way of giving departing ships the correct time in grand style. Built like much of the dock's architecture by Jesse Hartley in 1848, the granite tower is currently in need of some restoration but its Grade II listed status assures its protection and restoration is likely during the coming docks regeneration.

Tower Buildings

Completed in 1908 and designed by W. Aubury Thomas, the architectural style contrasts with his more famous work, the Liver Building. It was constructed with the then new steel frame construction technique, making this one of the earliest such buildings in the country. The building is clad in distinctive white Doulton terracotta to resist pollution.

Welsh Presbyterian Church

Not all Liverpool's architectural gems have been restored, and the Welsh Presbyterian Church, nicknamed the Toxteth Cathedral, awaits a bold restoration project. The church was designed by George and William Audsley and opened in 1868.

Town Hall

Left: The Town Hall was built in three stages, the original by John Wood built in 1749–54 with alterations by James Wyatt and John Foster in 1789–92. After a fire in 1795, it was rebuilt to what we see today. It was originally intended to be an exchange but was taken over by the corporation for municipal use following the fire.

Unity - Twin Towers

Built for Rumford Investments by structural engineers Faber Maunsell to a design by AHMM architects, the building comprises of two distinct parts: a 27-storey residential tower with a second 16-storey tower providing office accommodation. The residential tower features a dramatic two-storey penthouse pod, which is cantilevered out over the tower and is likely to be the city's most expensive apartment.

Beetham West Tower

Seen here nearing completion in spring 2007, the 40-storey, 140 metre tower was designed by Aedas AHR and cost £35 million. The building is mainly residential, with offices on the lower floors.

The White Star Line Head Office.

Opposite: Albion House was the head office for RMS *Titanic's* owners White Star Line. J. Bruce Ismay had his office in the corner closest to the camera. Built in 1898, it was designed by Richard Norman Shaw who also designed Scotland Yard in London. When the *Titanic* sank, large crowds gathered round the building while the names of the deceased were read from the balcony.

St Georges Hall

Built between 1841–51, the hall combined the requirement for a concert venue and law courts. Originally designed by Harvey Lonsdale Elmes, he died during its construction and the work was completed in 1855 by Robert Rawlinson and Charles Robert Cockerell. The court was in use until the new courts opened in 1984. The hall contains one of the largest organs in the UK, which was originally steam powered. Behind the hall is St John's Gardens, named after the church which stood on the site until 1887.

Wind Farm

Built on the edge of the Royal Seaforth Docks, the six 600kw wind turbines opened in 1999 producing 3.6MW of electricity in total, which is enough to power more than 2,000 homes. There are plans to increase this capacity in the near future with an additional five turbines. There is also a 25 turbine, 90MW offshore wind farm being built in Liverpool bay on the Burbo sandbank, 5.2km offshore from Crosby.

The Liverpool Institute

Opposite: Opened as the Liverpool Mechanics Institute in 1837, it is now the Liverpool Institute For Performing Arts. Paul McCartney and George Harrison both studied here, while John Lennon attended the nearby College of Art.

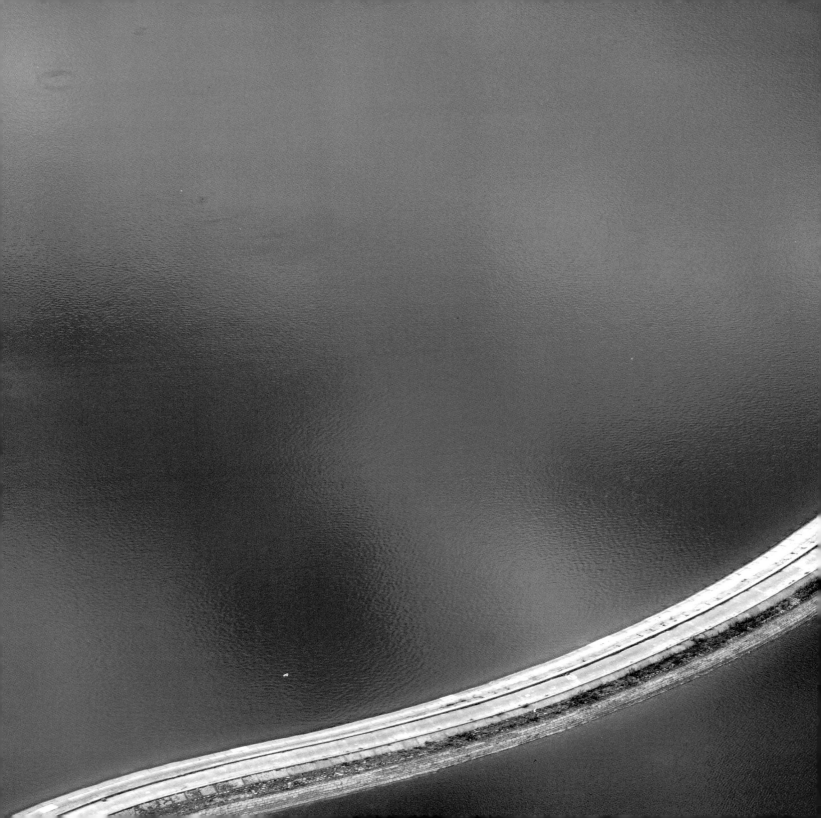

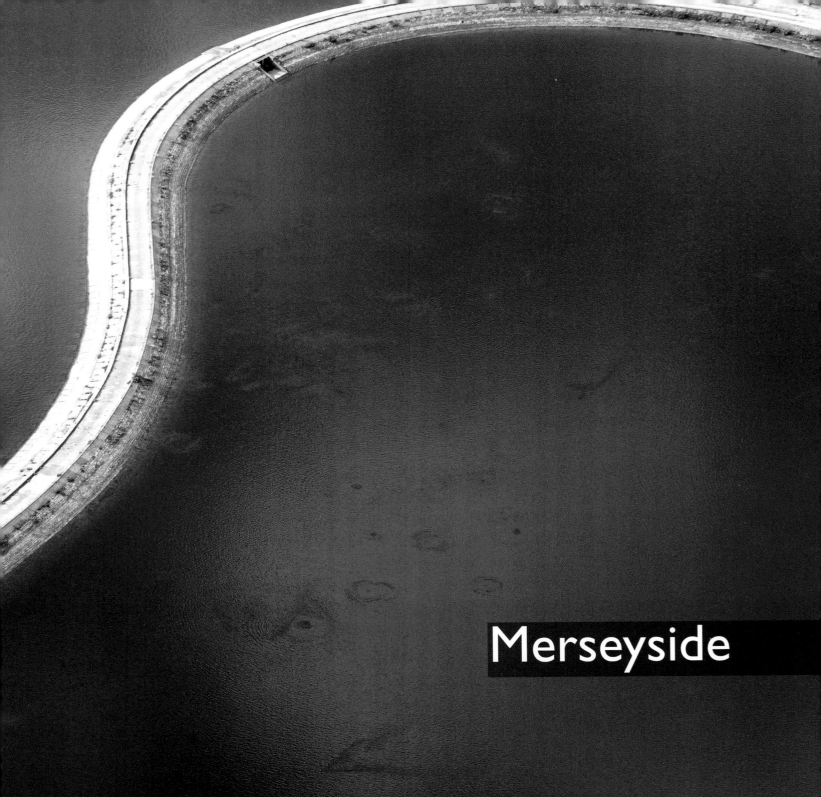

Merseyside

Bebington

Taken looking along the Wirral peninsular towards Birkenhead, this image shows the suburb of Bebington in the foreground with Liverpool city centre in the background on the right. Bebington's history goes back a long way - dinosaur footprints were found in the area!

Previous page: Prescot Reservoir

Hilbre Island

Lying just off the Wirral peninsular is Hilbre Island, which is a designated nature reserve. At low tide the island can be accessed by foot across the beach. The island is noted for its wildfowl and seals, although it also occasionally receives visits from whales and dolphins. Humans have visited the island since Neolithic times and it once had a Monastic Cell.

Sands of the Dee Estuary.

Wallasey

Up until the 19th century this was a sparsely-populated area, with the main activities being farming and fishing interspersed with occasional smuggling and wrecking. With the industrialisation of Liverpool and the coming of the steam ferry service, the area began to develop as a residential area for the affluent business people of the city. The area also took on a military role with the construction of Fort Perch Rock at the top right of the peninsular, which was built to defend the mouth of the Mersey Estuary. This area was also once home to the New Brighton Tower which was bigger and grander than the one at Blackpool but was unfortunately dismantled in the 1920s.

West Kirby

From the air, it is clear that the town is dominated by the striking marine lake that allows boats to sail at low tide. The world windsurfing speed record was broken on the lake at more than 42 knots. The photograph was taken on a very clear day and you can see right across the Wirral peninsular to Liverpool city centre.

Suburban

Bootle

The traditional home of dock workers and seamen, Bootle was also mentioned in the Domesday Book of 1086. In the first part of the 19th century, before the docks extended north, it was a bathing resort for the gentry of Liverpool.

Anfield

Left and previous page: Best known as the location of Liverpool Football Club's stadium, Anfield is also home to more than 15,000 people. Most of the housing is traditional terraced, which have proved ever popular despite plans to replace them with more modern houses. They continue to be sought after so much so that they more than doubled in value between 2001 and 2005.

Allerton

Much of the south of Liverpool is occupied by industry, as can be seen in this view taken from overhead Allerton looking south east towards Speke with Halewood and its famous car plant in the background left. Allerton itself is a very old settlement and was mentioned in the Domesday Book of 1086 as 'Alretun', which comes from the Anglo-Saxon meaning alder enclosure or farm.

The childhood homes of the Beatles' Paul McCartney and John Lennon are now preserved by the National Trust. The houses are open to the public via tours which start at the Albert Dock. John Lennon lived at 'Mendips'' and Paul McCartney lived at Forthlin Road.

Above: 20 Forthlin Road.
Left: 'Mendips' 251 Menlove Avenue.

Molyneux Road, Kensington

Known locally as 'Kenny' the Kensington area of Liverpool lies just east of the city centre and is noted for its high concentration of traditional Victorian terraced houses, which make a fascinating picture from above. The area has recently benefited from some considerable investment in the Kensington Regeneration plan.

Litherland

Litherland is a district of Sefton and lies to the north of the Liverpool urban area. In the foreground of the image is Rimrose Valley Country Park, adjacent to which you can see part of the Leeds to Liverpool Canal. In the background right is Winter Hill with its television transmitter aerial.

Penny Lane

Penny Lane was made famous in the Beatles song of 1967 and has remained a popular tourist destination ever since. The Beatles' John Lennon and Paul McCartney grew up in the area and their nearby childhood homes are preserved as museums. It took quite some time to get this image with a perfect 'blue suburban sky' as the song puts it. The road is named after James Penny, an 18th century slave trader.

Toxteth

The Welsh Streets area of Toxteth are 19th century terraced houses, built from Welsh brick to house Welsh dock workers, and all the streets carry Welsh names. The area is currently under threat of demolition, with a plan to replace the homes with more modern buildings. Nine Madryn Street (the upper most shown in its entirety above) was the birthplace of the Beatles' Ringo Starr.

Above: Aigburth Road, Aigburth.

Opposite: Restoration of terraced houses on Tancred Road. The housing stock of many parts of the city are being renewed. Sometimes this involves demolition, but occasionally the existing houses are being refurbished to rejuvenate the housing market in the more depressed areas.

Commerce

Ranelagh Street

Lying in the heart of the retail district in the city centre, Ranelagh Street is alive with the hustle and bustle of shoppers visiting a full range of traders, from market stalls to the Clayton Square Shopping Centre behind.

Previous page: Market on London Road.

Lord Street

The first warm days of spring bring out the shoppers in droves, eager to shake off the winter blues with some retail therapy. The roadworks are part of a £73 million scheme to improve the roads, streets and public spaces in the city centre.

Royal Insurance Building

Built in 1897–1903 to a design by J. Francis Doyle, the grand Baroque style of the Grade II listed building reflects the prestige and importance of the insurance trade in the city and is one of the earliest uses of steel frame construction in the country.

Church Street

Taking its name from St Peter's Church, Church Street is at the heart of the shopping area, indeed, St Peter's was demolished in 1923 to make way for more shops. The church was opened in 1704 and stood on a site in the centre of this image on the left-hand side of the street. In the top left corner we can see work progressing on the Paradise Street project, which will greatly expand the retail capacity of the area. Note the excellent provision of public transport with the number of buses and taxis travelling along Hanover Street in the bottom of the image.

Old Hall Street

Old Hall Street showing the newly-completed Unity Twin Towers building on the left, the reconstruction of Exchange Flags in the bottom foreground and Liverpool's tallest building, the Beetham West Tower, nearing completion at the top left. Of particular interest on the right is the former Exchange Station opened in 1850 and closed in 1977, when the station was replaced by the underground. The original station façade has been incorporated into a new office complex.

Williamson Square

Recently rebuilt as part of a £5.75 million upgrade scheme, the square now features this spectacular fountain with 20 computer controlled jets which create a double arch of water with differing displays up to four metres high.

Transport

Railway

Opened in 1830, the Liverpool and Manchester Railway was the world's first passenger railway, with its Liverpool terminus here at Crown Street Station. The railway was so popular that soon after its opening a new larger station had to be built at Lime Street, which involved digging these cuttings (right) by hand which are still in use 170 years later. When passenger handling moved to Lime Street, Crown Street station was used for goods right up to 1972. Although the site has been landscaped, the original 1830s entrance tunnel is still there, buried adjacent to the 1840s tunnel you can see in the image, which is still used occasionally for shunting.

Previous page: Lime Street Station.

Right: Railway cutting, Lime Street Station approach.

Lime Street Station

Opened in 1836, the first of the glass and iron roofs was added in 1849 and was the largest iron roof in existence at the time. The station's most distinctive feature, the Great North Western Hotel, was completed in 1867 to a design by Alfred Waterhouse. Although it is no longer a hotel, the building is still in use providing student accommodation for the nearby university. The second iron and glass roof was added in the 1880s, and in the 1970s and underground station was added connecting it to the Liverpool Loop underground line.

Old Liverpool Airport

Officially opened in 1933, flights from the then-named Speke Airport actually began three years before in 1930. A new runway was added adjacent to the original airport in 1966 and 20 years later a new terminal was built, taking operations away from the original site. The Grade II listed 1930s art deco terminal is now used as a hotel.

Queens Square Bus Station

Liverpool, in common with many other UK cities, has been keen to promote the use of public transport as opposed to private cars and as such has made considerable investment in the infrastructure to achieve this.

John Lennon Airport

In 2002 Speke Airport was renamed the Liverpool John Lennon Airport, in honour of the late Beatles member. In recent years passenger numbers have grown with the boom in no frills airlines such as Easy Jet. For little more than the price of this book, one can fly from here to continental cities such as Cologne. This has opened up a huge potential for business and social possibilities, both of which this author has particularly benefitted from.

Leeds - Liverpool Canal

At 127 miles, the canal is the longest in the country and allows through traffic from the Irish Sea to the North Sea. The canal was fully opened in 1816, having taken 46 years to complete. The locks lead to Stanley Dock, through which the Mersey and Irish Sea can be reached. The stub used to go some three miles further but that end is now infilled.

George's Dock Ventilation Tower

Built in 1934, the Art Deco Mersey Road Tunnel Ventilation Tower was designed by Herbert J. Rowse. The tower is Grade II listed and the base of the building contains the tunnel offices.

Left: Construction of the new canal link at Pier Head, which will allow canal access between the north and south docks. The construction work has uncovered some of the original dock walls and lock gates previously buried.

The Queensway Tunnel

Again designed by Herbert J. Rowse, the Queensway Tunnel has been given a grand entrance which is now Grade II listed. The road tunnel was opened in 1934 to supplement the ferry service and the rail tunnel, which had been built in 1886. Increasing traffic meant that it also had to be supplemented by a second tunnel opened in 1971.